LIVE IT:
EMPATHY

MARTHA MARTIN

Crabtree Publishing Company
www.crabtreebooks.com

Author: Martha Martin
Coordinating editor: Bonnie Dobkin
Publishing plan research and development:
    Sean Charlebois, Reagan Miller
    Crabtree Publishing Company
Editor: Reagan Miller
Proofreader: Crystal Sikkens
Editorial director: Kathy Middleton
Production coordinator: Margaret Salter
Prepress technician: Margaret Salter

Logo design: Samantha Crabtree
Project Manager: Santosh Vasudevan (Q2AMEDIA)
Art Direction: Rahul Dhiman (Q2AMEDIA)
Design: Neha Kaul and Parul Gambhir (Q2AMEDIA)
Illustrations: Q2AMEDIA
Front Cover: Six-year-old Hannah Turner is thanked for
    helping homeless people stay warm through her
    organziation "Hannah's Socks."
Title Page: Dan Rooney helps the son of a fallen U.S. soldier
    receive a scholarship for his education.

Library and Archives Canada Cataloguing in Publication

Martin, Martha, 1967-
    Live it: empathy / Martha Martin.

(Crabtree character sketches)
Includes index.
ISBN 978-0-7787-4882-3 (bound).--ISBN 978-0-7787-4915-8 (pbk.)

    1. Empathy--Juvenile literature. 2. Biography--Juvenile literature.
I. Title. II. Title: Empathy. III. Series: Crabtree character sketches

BF575.E55M37 2010   j177'.7   C2009-905515-5

Library of Congress Cataloging-in-Publication Data

Martin, Martha
    Live it. Empathy / Martha Martin.
       p. cm. -- (Crabtree character sketches)
    Includes index.
    ISBN 978-0-7787-4915-8 (pbk. : alk. paper) -- ISBN 978-0-7787-4882-3
(reinforced library binding : alk. paper)

    1. Empathy--Juvenile literature. 2. Sympathy--Juvenile literature. 3.
Conduct of life--Juvenile literature. I. Title. II. Title: Empathy.
    BJ1475.M93 2010
    177'.7--dc22

                                                  2009036855

Crabtree Publishing Company

Printed in the USA/122009/BG20090930

www.crabtreebooks.com   1-800-387-7650

Published in Canada
Crabtree Publishing
616 Welland Ave.
St. Catharines, ON
L2M 5V6

Published in the United States
Crabtree Publishing
PMB 59051
350 Fifth Avenue, 59th Floor
New York, New York 10118

Published in the United Kingdom
Crabtree Publishing
Maritime House
Basin Road North, Hove
BN41 1WR

Published in Australia
Crabtree Publishing
386 Mt. Alexander Rd.
Ascot Vale (Melbourne)
VIC 3032

CONTENTS

WHAT IS EMPATHY?

EMPATHY IS WHAT HAPPENS WHEN YOU TRY TO UNDERSTAND WHAT SOMEONE ELSE IS FEELING—EVEN IF YOU DON'T FEEL THE SAME WAY. IN THIS BOOK, YOU'LL MEET SOME REAL EMPATHY SUPERSTARS. THEY SHOW US THAT THINKING ABOUT OTHERS ALSO MAKES YOU FEEL BETTER ABOUT YOURSELF.

LIAM ANDREWS AND JORDAN THORNE
HELPED HIS BEST FRIEND DEAL WITH CANCER

SUSAN FYFE
FOUNDER OF
"THE RESCUE 100 FOUNDATION"

DAN ROONEY
CREATOR OF "FOLDS OF HONOR" FOUNDATION
AND PATRIOT GOLF DAY

HANNAH TURNER
OHIO SCHOOL GIRL AND INSPIRATION
FOR "HANNAH'S SOCKS."

ERIC WALTERS
CHILDREN'S AUTHOR AND PROMOTER FOR
"CREATION OF HOPE"

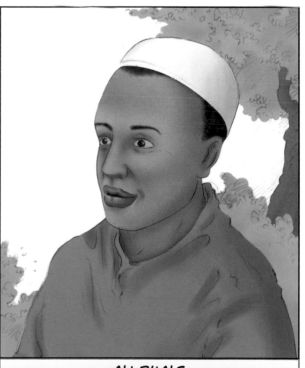

ALI DUALE
HALIFAX FIREFIGHTER
AND FRIEND TO IMMIGRANT YOUTH

EMPATHY FOR THE SICK

LIAM ANDREWS

WHO IS HE?
A SOCCER-PLAYING TEEN FROM BRISTOL, ENGLAND

WHY HIM?
WHEN LIAM HEARD HIS BEST FRIEND, JORDAN THORNE, WAS LOSING HIS HAIR FROM CANCER, LIAM FOUND AN UNUSUAL WAY TO SUPPORT HIM.

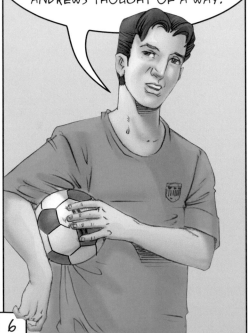

DO YOU HAVE A GOOD FRIEND, SOMEONE YOU'VE KNOWN FOR YEARS? WHEN A FRIEND IS GOING THROUGH A DIFFICULT TIME, HOW CAN YOU SHOW YOU CARE? LIAM ANDREWS THOUGHT OF A WAY.

FALL 2007, BRISTOL ENGLAND

THAT WAS A GREAT SHOT, JORDAN! WELL DONE!

WHAT DO YOU MEAN, "WELL DONE?" THAT GOAL INTO THE TOP CORNER WAS WICKED!

YOU'VE GOT A GREAT CAREER AHEAD OF YOU IN SPORTS, JORDAN! MAYBE YOU'LL EVEN PLAY FOR MANCHESTER UNITED SOME DAY!

THANKS, COACH! THAT'S MY GOAL!

JORDAN SEEMED HEADED FOR A BRIGHT FUTURE.

I THINK IT'S GREAT YOU GOT ONTO THE BRISTOL ROVERS TEAM, JORDAN!

YOU'VE GOT TO GET ON, TOO.

NEXT TRIALS ARE IN THE FALL! IN THE MEANTIME, WE'LL KEEP PRACTICING!

BUT THEN ONE DAY...

JORDAN! WHAT HAPPENED? WHY DID YOU ASK TO BE SUBSTITUTED? THE TEAM NEEDS YOU AND THAT LEFT FOOT OF YOURS!

MY BACK HURTS, COACH, AND I FEEL LIKE I CAN'T BREATHE.

I JUST DON'T FEEL RIGHT...

WELL, TAKE IT EASY. I'LL HAVE THE TEAM DOCTOR LOOK AT YOU.

BUT IT WAS SOON CLEAR THAT THIS WAS MORE THAN A SPORTS INJURY.

I'M SO SORRY. I'M AFRAID JORDAN HAS A RARE FORM OF CANCER, *EWING'S CARCINOMA*. IT TENDS TO STRIKE YOUNG PEOPLE.

JORDAN SHARED THE NEWS WITH LIAM.

YOU KNOW HOW I HAVEN'T BEEN FEELING TOO WELL LATELY? IT TURNS OUT, I'VE GOT CANCER. I HAVE TO HAVE **CHEMO** AND **RADIATION** TREATMENTS.

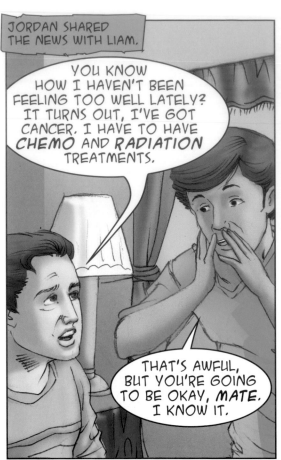

THAT'S AWFUL, BUT YOU'RE GOING TO BE OKAY, **MATE.** I KNOW IT.

JORDAN'S GOING TO LOSE HIS HAIR WITH THE CHEMO, MOM. I WAS THINKING... MAYBE I'LL GET MY HEAD SHAVED. YOU KNOW, TO KEEP HIM COMPANY.

YOU'RE A GOOD FRIEND, LI! MAYBE YOU CAN EVEN GET PEOPLE TO SPONSOR YOU. THEN YOU CAN DONATE THE MONEY TO CANCER RESEARCH.

WAIT 'TIL I TELL JORDAN!

I THINK I'LL GROW MY HAIR LONGER. MAYBE I'LL EVEN GROW A **GOATEE!**

A FEW MONTHS LATER.

I CAN'T BELIEVE ALL THE **DONATIONS,** LI! AND SOMEONE'S GIVING **60 POUNDS*** JUST SO YOU'LL GET RID OF THAT UGLY GOATEE?

YEAH, IT WAS PROBABLY MY MOM.

*$100 DOLLARS

LIAM DECIDED TO HOLD THE BIG SHAVE-OFF AT HIS SCHOOL, IN FRONT OF ALL HIS CLASSMATES. THE LOCAL REPORTERS WERE ALSO THERE.

LIAM, TELL US WHY YOU ARE DOING THIS.

BECAUSE JORDAN'S MY BEST MATE. I DON'T WANT HIM TO FEEL DIFFERENT.

BACK AT JORDAN'S HOUSE.

YOU LOOK FANTASTIC. THANKS A LOT, MATE!

ANYTHING FOR YOU, MATE.

JORDAN RESPONDED WELL TO TREATMENT AND WAS SOON BACK ON THE FIELD WITH HIS FRIEND. LIAM'S EMPATHY AND SUPPORT MAY HAVE HELPED ALMOST AS MUCH AS THE MEDICINE!

WHAT IF ONE OF YOUR FRIENDS WAS IN NEED OF YOUR SUPPORT? WOULD YOU BE THE KIND OF FRIEND LIAM WAS?

WHAT WOULD YOU DO?

IMAGINE A FRIEND OF YOURS HAS LOST SOMEONE IN HER FAMILY TO A TERRIBLE ILLNESS. YOU TRY TO COMFORT HER, BUT YOU REALIZE THE HEALING PROCESS WILL TAKE A LONG TIME.

HOW DO YOU THINK YOUR FRIEND IS FEELING? WHAT COULD YOU DO TO MAKE HER FEEL BETTER?

EMPATHY FOR ANIMALS

WHO IS SHE?
A NURSE AND A STABLE OWNER FROM ALBERTA, CANADA

WHY HER?
SUSAN RESCUED 100 ABUSED AND NEGLECTED **ARABIAN** HORSES. SHE ALSO STARTED "THE RESCUE 100 FOUNDATION."

WE ALL CARE ABOUT OUR OWN PETS, AND WE FEEL AWFUL WHEN WE HEAR ABOUT AN ANIMAL THAT HAS BEEN HURT OR BADLY TREATED. BUT HOW MANY OF US DO SOMETHING?

WHEN SUSAN FYFE LEARNED ABOUT A HERD OF ABUSED HORSES, SHE DID MORE THAN JUST GET UPSET. SHE DECIDED TO HELP. HOW MANY OF US WOULD DO SOMETHING ABOUT IT?

SUSAN FYFE IS A NURSE. SHE IS ALSO A MOTHER OF FOUR, A PUBLIC SPEAKER, AND A STABLE OWNER. SHE LOVES THE HORSES AS IF THEY WERE HER CHILDREN.

SO, HOW ARE MY GIRLS TODAY?

ON A MONDAY IN MARCH, 2008, SUSAN RETURNED FROM A TRIP TO FIND PEOPLE BUZZING WITH NEWS.

HORSES? WHAT HORSES?

DID YOU HEAR ABOUT THOSE HORSES? IT'S JUST TRAGIC.

WHEN SUSAN GOT HOME, SHE SAW AN ARTICLE THAT HER FATHER HAD LEFT FOR HER.

"HORSES RESCUED..." THIS MUST BE WHAT EVERYONE WAS TALKING ABOUT!

"OVER 100 ARABIAN HORSES HAVE BEEN RESCUED FROM A FARM NORTHEAST OF EDMONTON, ALBERTA. THEY HAD ALL BEEN STARVED, ABUSED, AND NEGLECTED. ANOTHER 27 WERE ALREADY DEAD."

I CAN'T BELIEVE THIS...

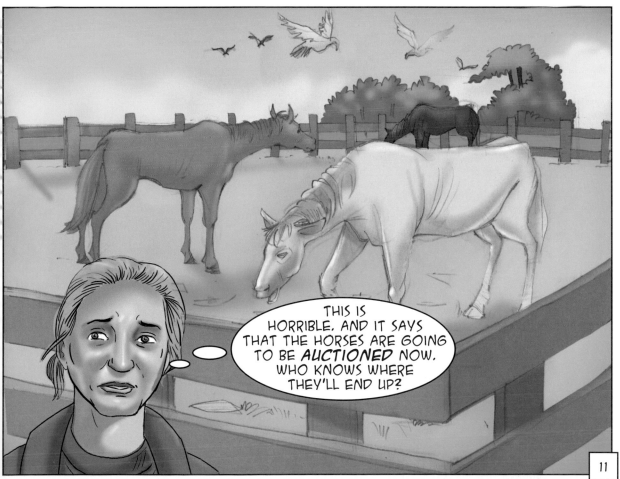

THIS IS HORRIBLE. AND IT SAYS THAT THE HORSES ARE GOING TO BE AUCTIONED NOW. WHO KNOWS WHERE THEY'LL END UP?

IT TOOK MONTHS OF CARE...

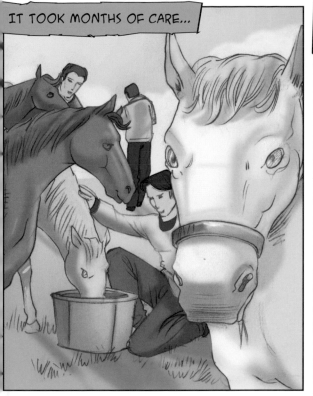

...BUT EVENTUALLY THE HORSES WERE HEALTHY AGAIN. SUSAN MADE SURE EACH FOUND A GOOD HOME.

THIS IS THE LAST ONE TO BE ADOPTED. JUST LOOK HOW BEAUTIFUL AND HEALTHY HE IS.

WE DID A GOOD THING, EVERYONE.

WITHIN MONTHS, SUSAN AND HER FRIENDS STARTED "THE RESCUE 100 FOUNDATION." THEY MAKE SURE OTHER ANIMALS CONTINUE TO GET THE HELP THEY NEED.

SUSAN FYFE'S EMPATHY MADE A LIFE-AND-DEATH DIFFERENCE TO THE HORSES. SUSAN DIDN'T WAIT FOR OTHERS TO GET THE JOB DONE—SHE GOT INVOLVED HERSELF.

WHAT WOULD YOU DO?

YOU'RE WALKING HOME FROM SCHOOL, AND YOU PASS A GATE THAT HAS BEEN LEFT OPEN. GLANCING INSIDE, YOU NOTICE A DOZEN DOGS CHAINED TO STAKES IN THE FENCED BACK YARD. THE DOGS LOOK SICK.

HOW WOULD YOU REACT? IS THERE SOMETHING YOU COULD DO? SHOULD YOU EVEN GET INVOLVED?

EMPATHY FOR THOSE SUFFERING A LOSS

DAN ROONEY

WHO IS HE?
A U.S. FIGHTER PILOT—AND A GOLF PRO

WHY HIM?
DAN STARTED THE "FOLDS OF HONOR" FOUNDATION AND PATRIOT GOLF DAY.

AS A FIGHTER PILOT IN IRAQ, DAN ROONEY OFTEN WONDERED WHAT WOULD HAPPEN TO HIS FAMILY IF HE DIDN'T COME BACK FROM THE WAR.

MAYBE THIS IS WHY DAN FELT EMPATHY FOR THE FAMILIES OF OTHER SOLDIERS. SEE WHAT HE DID TO HELP THEM.

THE WAR IN IRAQ

A FEW MORE MISSIONS AND I'LL BE HOME AGAIN. THIS SECOND TOUR OF DUTY HAS SEEMED SO LONG...

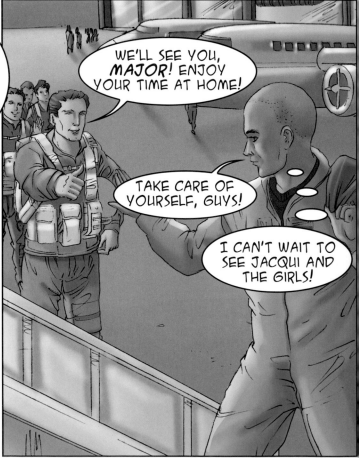

WE'LL SEE YOU, *MAJOR!* ENJOY YOUR TIME AT HOME!

TAKE CARE OF YOURSELF, GUYS!

I CAN'T WAIT TO SEE JACQUI AND THE GIRLS!

IT COULD HAVE BEEN ME COMING HOME IN A COFFIN. THERE MUST BE SOMETHING I CAN DO TO HELP THE FAMILIES OF THESE FALLEN SOLDIERS....

SAFELY BACK AT HOME, DAN QUICKLY CAME UP WITH A PLAN.

I WANT TO RAISE SOME MONEY TO HELP THE FAMILIES OF MICHIGAN'S FALLEN HEROES. AND SINCE GOLF IS WHAT I KNOW...

IN NO TIME, DAN HAD ORGANIZED A FUNDRAISER.

WELCOME TO THE WEST MICHIGAN FALLEN HEROES GOLF **TOURNAMENT!** ALL PROCEEDS WILL GO TO A WONDERFUL CAUSE— TO PROVIDE **SCHOLARSHIPS** FOR THE CHILDREN OF OUR FALLEN SOLDIERS.

GRAND HEAVEN GOLF CLUB

THE MICHIGAN TOURNAMENT WAS A HUGE SUCCESS. SO DAN APPROACHED MEMBERS OF THE **PGA** WITH AN EVEN BIGGER IDEA...

I WANT TO PROVIDE SCHOLARSHIPS FOR THE FAMILIES OF ALL OUR FALLEN HEROES. WE'LL CALL THE ORGANIZATION "FOLDS OF HONOR."

NOT LONG AFTERWARDS...

ON BEHALF OF "FOLDS OF HONOR", I'M PROUD TO WELCOME YOU TO THE FIRST EVER PATRIOT GOLF DAY! THANKS FOR SUPPORTING OUR SOLDIERS AND THEIR FAMILIES.

THANK YOU SO MUCH! WITHOUT YOUR HELP, I'M NOT SURE WE WOULD EVER HAVE BEEN ABLE TO SEND BROCK'S SON TO COLLEGE.

DON'T THANK ME. IT'S WHAT I'D WANT DONE FOR MY OWN FAMILY.

ANOTHER TOUR OF DUTY IN IRAQ... PLEASE, DAN. STAY SAFE. PROMISE.

I PROMISE, SWEETHEART.

AND NOW I KNOW YOU KNOW YOU AND THE GIRLS WILL BE TAKEN CARE OF...

NO MATTER WHAT.

THE FIRST PATRIOT GOLF DAY RAISED OVER $1,000,000, AND FOLDS OF HONOR DONATED OVER **200** SCHOLARSHIPS TO FAMILIES OF FALLEN HEROES. THE NUMBERS GO UP EVERY YEAR.

DAN ROONEY'S EMPATHY FOR A LITTLE BOY STANDING BESIDE HIS FATHER'S COFFIN CHANGED MANY LIVES. DAN UNDERSTOOD WHAT THAT LITTLE BOY HAD LOST... AND HE DID WHAT HE COULD TO HELP.

WHAT WOULD YOU DO?

THE FAMILIES OF SOLDIERS NEED OUR SUPPORT AND HELP. BUT THE SOLDIERS THEMSELVES NEED US, TOO. THEY ARE OFTEN IN A STRANGE COUNTRY AND MISSING THE ONES THEY LOVE.

HOW COULD YOU SHOW THE SOLDIERS THAT YOU UNDERSTAND WHAT THEY'RE FEELING? WHAT COULD YOU DO TO SUPPORT THEM?

EMPATHY FOR THOSE IN NEED

HANNAH TURNER

WHO IS SHE?
A LITTLE GIRL FROM OHIO

WHY HER?
HANNAH WAS ONLY FOUR YEARS OLD WHEN HER EMPATHY FOR *A HOMELESS* MAN STARTED CHANGING LIVES.

YOU DON'T HAVE TO BE AN ADULT TO MAKE A DIFFERENCE, AND YOU DON'T NEED A LOT OF MONEY. EVEN THOUGH SHE WAS JUST A LITTLE GIRL, HANNAH'S EMPATHY HELPED HER SEE A SIMPLE NEED THAT OTHER PEOPLE HAD MISSED.

IN 2004, HANNAH TURNER WAS A TYPICAL FOUR-YEAR-OLD GIRL, LIVING HAPPILY IN PERRYSBURG, OHIO.

SHE CAME FROM A LARGE FAMILY AND HAD EVERYTHING SHE NEEDED.

DON'T RUN SO FAST! I CAN'T CATCH YOU!

WHO'S READY FOR MORE FOOD?

YOU'RE NOT SUPPOSED TO CATCH ME!

BUT HANNAH'S FAMILY NEVER FORGOT THAT OTHERS WEREN'T AS FORTUNATE...

THERE'S NO BETTER WAY TO SPEND THANKSGIVING THAN HERE AT THE CHERRY STREET *MISSION.*

MOMMY SAID ALL THESE PEOPLE DON'T HAVE PLACES TO LIVE. HOW DO THEY STAY WARM?

MOMMY, THAT MAN HAS OLD SHOES, AND NO SOCKS. WON'T HIS FEET GET COLD?

HIS SHOES WILL KEEP HIS TOES WARM, HONEY.

BUT HANNAH WASN'T CONVINCED...

HE CAN HAVE MY SOCKS!

19

NO, SWEETIE, STOP. YOUR SOCKS WON'T FIT HIM.

BUT...

I PROMISE, HANNAH. WE'LL GET SOME SOCKS FOR HIM TOMORROW.

THE NEXT DAY, DORIS AND THE EIGHT TURNER KIDS BOUGHT EVERY PAIR OF SOCKS THEY COULD FIND.

I THINK WE FOUND OVER 100 PAIRS OF SOCKS! THAT WILL KEEP A LOT OF PEOPLE'S FEET WARM, HANNAH!

CAN WE TAKE THEM TO THAT MAN, NOW?

THE TURNER FAMILY DELIVERED THEIR DONATION TO THE MISSION.

WE CAN'T THANK YOU ENOUGH! NO ONE EVER THINKS ABOUT GIVING US SOCKS OR UNDERWEAR!

YOUR DONATION WILL HELP A LOT OF PEOPLE.

YOU SHOULD HAVE SEEN THE REACTION! IT'S GOING TO MAKE SUCH A DIFFERENCE. AND COLLECTING SOCKS—IT ISN'T HARD TO DO.

SO LET'S FIGURE OUT HOW WE CAN DO MORE.

AND THEY DID.

FOR TWO YEARS, WE BOUGHT SOCKS ON OUR OWN AND GAVE THEM TO **SHELTERS**. NOW WE'VE STARTED AN ORGANIZATION, WHICH WE'RE CALLING "HANNAH'S SOCKS."

AND IT ALL STARTED WITH A LITTLE GIRL.

YES, IT DID. AND IF EVERYONE CARED AS MUCH AS HANNAH... IF EVERYONE REACHED OUT...*

*ACTUAL QUOTE

SINCE YOU STARTED "HANNAH'S SOCKS," PEOPLE IN SHELTERS ACROSS THE STATE HAVE WARM SOCKS AND CLOTHING. YOU'VE REALLY HELPED A LOT OF PEOPLE, HANNAH.

AND WE'RE GOING TO KEEP ON HELPING, TOO!

"HANNAH'S SOCKS" BEGAN WITH THE EMPATHY OF ONE LITTLE GIRL. BY THINKING ABOUT SOMEONE ELSE, SHE'S NOW MADE LIFE A LITTLE BETTER FOR THOUSANDS OF PEOPLE.

HOW WOULD YOU REACT IF YOU SAW SOMEONE IN NEED?

WHAT WOULD YOU DO?

IMAGINE YOU AND YOUR FRIEND ARE WALKING DOWN A STREET NEAR YOUR HOME.

YOU PASS A LOCAL FOOD SHELTER. OUTSIDE IS A SIGN: "CANNED GOODS AND BOXED FOOD ITEMS NEEDED. INFORMATION INSIDE." YOUR FRIEND GLANCES AT IT AND KEEPS WALKING. WHAT COULD YOU SUGGEST THE TWO OF YOU DO, INSTEAD?

EMPATHY FOR THOSE IN OTHER LANDS

ERIC WALTERS

WHO IS HE?
AN AWARD-WINNING CHILDREN'S AUTHOR

WHY HIM?
ERIC FELT EMPATHY FOR PEOPLE IN ANOTHER COUNTRY, AND DID SOMETHING TO HELP THEM.

WE'D ALL LIKE TO THINK WE'D HELP SOMEONE IN NEED. BUT HOW MANY OF US REALLY WOULD?

ERIC WALTERS SAW SOME UPSETTING THINGS WHEN HE WAS IN KENYA. HE COULD HAVE JUST RETURNED HOME AND FORGOTTEN ABOUT THEM. INSTEAD, HE DECIDED TO MAKE A DIFFERENCE.

ERIC WALTERS WAS VISITING KENYA, AFRICA, WITH HIS SON, NICHOLAS. NICHOLAS HAD RAISED $20,000 TO HELP BUILD A SCHOOL IN HONOR OF HIS UNCLE PETER, WHO HAD DIED OF CANCER.

KENYA IS SO BEAUTIFUL. UNCLE PETER WOULD HAVE LOVED IT.

WELL, MAYBE PART OF HIM WILL BE HERE IN THE SCHOOL WE'RE BUILDING.

ERIC AND HIS SON GOT TO KNOW THE LOCAL PEOPLE. THEY ESPECIALLY ENJOYED MEETING THE CHILDREN.

HEADS UP!

IN AUGUST **2008**, THE COMMUNITY IN KIKIMA CAME TOGETHER TO BREAK GROUND FOR A NEW CHILDREN'S RESIDENCE.

THANKS TO THE SUCCESS OF ERIC'S PROGRAM, CHILDREN LIKE MUKUTU REALLY DO HAVE REASON TO BE HOPEFUL ABOUT THE FUTURE.

ERIC WALTERS FELT EMPATHY FOR THE PEOPLE OF KIKIMA. HE SAW THINGS THROUGH THEIR EYES, AND THROUGH THE EYES OF HIS FRIENDS.

NOW, HE AND HIS PARTNERS ARE HELPING AN ENTIRE VILLAGE. IT'S PRETTY AMAZING WHAT CAN BE ACCOMPLISHED BY PEOPLE WHO CARE!

WHAT WOULD YOU DO?

IT'S BEEN RAINING FOR DAYS. A RIVER NEARBY HAS OVERFLOWED, AND SURROUNDING AREAS ARE FLOODING. YOU SEE PICTURES ON THE NEWS OF FAMILIES JUST LIKE YOURS LEAVING THEIR HOMES, OR WATCHING THEIR BELONGINGS FLOAT AWAY.

YOU THINK ABOUT HOW YOU WOULD FEEL IN THAT SITUATION. IS THERE ANYTHING YOU COULD DO TO HELP?

EMPATHY FOR NEWCOMERS

ALI DUALE

WHO IS HE?
A HALIFAX FIREFIGHTER AND A **REFUGEE** FROM **SOMALIA**

WHY HIM?
HE STARTED A CLUB FOR IMMIGRANT CHILDREN.

WE ALL KNOW WHAT IT'S LIKE TO GO SOMEPLACE NEW. MAYBE IT'S BEEN A NEW SCHOOL, A NEW HOUSE, OR A NEW CITY. IT TAKES A WHILE TO FEEL AS THOUGH YOU BELONG.

ALI DUALE LEARNED ABOUT FITTING IN WHEN HIS FAMILY MOVED TO CANADA FROM SOMALIA. READ HOW HE HELPED MAKE THE EXPERIENCE EASIER FOR OTHERS.

BACK IN THE 1990'S, ALI WAS A REFUGEE FROM THE **CIVIL WAR** IN SOMALIA, LIVING IN A REFUGEE CAMP.

WE HAVE BEEN HERE FOR SEVEN YEARS NOW. HOW MUCH LONGER WILL WE HAVE TO STAY?

MY FAMILY SHOULD NOT BE LIVING IN A CARDBOARD SHACK. THERE IS NO ROOM... NO RUNNING WATER... NO BATHROOM.

AT LEAST MY WIFE AND CHILDREN ARE WITH ME, AND WE ARE SAFE FROM THE DANGERS IN OUR COUNTRY...MORE OR LESS.

FINALLY, IN *1997*, THEY RECEIVED WONDERFUL NEWS!

CANADA WILL GIVE US REFUGE! THEY WILL ALLOW US TO COME TO THEIR COUNTRY!

REALLY? THIS IS WONDERFUL. PRAISE *ALLAH!*

THEY ARRIVED IN HALIFAX, NOVA SCOTIA.

WELCOME TO YOUR NEW COUNTRY, CHILDREN!

I'M SCARED, MAMA.

BUT NO ONE HERE TALKS LIKE US, AND THEY ALL LOOK DIFFERENT.

I KNOW HOW MY CHILDREN FEEL—LIKE WE DO NOT BELONG.

BUT ALI WAS DETERMINED THAT THEY WOULD FIT IN. HE WENT TO A SCHOOL FOR NEWCOMERS.

HE BECAME A FIREFIGHTER.

AND HE WOULDN'T LET HIS CHILDREN GIVE UP.

GO JOIN THOSE BOYS. YOU'LL NEVER FIT IN HERE IF YOU DON'T TRY.

27

ALI ORGANIZED THE "SUNDAY NIGHT CLUB" AT THE LOCAL COMMUNITY CENTER. IT WAS A HUGE HIT!

SOON THEY WILL ALL FEEL THEY BELONG. I AM GLAD I HAVE THE CHANCE TO DO THIS THING FOR MY COMMUNITY.*

* ACTUAL QUOTE

ALI DUALE KNEW HOW KIDS FELT COMING TO A NEW PLACE. HE'D FELT THE SAME WAY HIMSELF...AND HE WAS AN ADULT!

ALI FELT EMPATHY FOR THE NEWCOMERS HE SAW—AND HE FOUND A WAY TO MAKE THE JOURNEY EASIER!

YOU CAN'T PUT A PRICE TAG ON THAT.*

* ACTUAL QUOTE

WHAT WOULD YOU DO?

SCHOOL HAS JUST BEGUN FOR THE DAY. YOUR TEACHER WALKS IN WITH A SCARED-LOOKING GIRL.

"THIS IS POULOMI," SAYS YOUR TEACHER. "SHE JUST MOVED HERE A FEW DAYS AGO."

THE GIRL LOWERS HER EYES. WHAT COULD YOU DO TO HELP THIS NEWCOMER ADJUST?

WEB SITES

RESCUE *100* IS THE FOUNDATION SUSAN FYFE BEGAN AS A WAY OF CARING FOR NEGLECTED AND ABUSED ANIMALS.

www.rescue100.com

"FOLDS OF HONOR" BEGAN AS A WAY FOR DAN ROONEY TO SHOW EMPATHY TO THE FAMILIES OF HEROES.

www.foldsofhonor.com

THE "CREATION OF HOPE" PROJECT IS MAKING A DIFFERENCE IN THE LIVES OF THE PEOPLE OF KIKIMA.

www.hwdsb.on.ca/community/hope/index.aspx

WHEN HANNAH TURNER OFFERED HER OWN SOCKS TO A HOMELESS MAN IN OHIO, HER EMPATHY MOVED OTHERS TO DO THE SAME.

www.hannahssocks.org

GLOSSARY

ALLAH THE NAME FOR GOD IN ISLAM

ARABIAN A BREED OF HORSE THAT STARTED IN THE ORIENT, BUT IS NOW FOUND ALL OVER THE WORLD

AUCTIONED SOLD TO THE PERSON OFFERING THE HIGHEST AMOUNT OF MONEY AT A SPECIFIC TIME

CHEMO CHEMOTHERAPY; A CANCER TREATMENT WHERE A PATIENT IS INJECTED WITH CHEMICALS TO KILL THE DISEASE. LOSS OF HAIR IS A COMMON SIDE EFFECT

CIVIL WAR A WAR BETWEEN OPPOSING GROUPS OF PEOPLE FROM THE SAME COUNTRY OR REGION

DONATION A GIFT OF MONEY OR SOMETHING VALUABLE TO HELP OTHERS

EWING'S CARCINOMA A CANCER THAT STARTS IN THE BONES OR TISSUES OF THE BODY

FARRIER A PERSON WHO TRIMS AND SHOES HORSES' HOOVES

GOATEE A SMALL BEARD ON THE CHIN

HOMELESS SOMEONE WHO HAS NO PLACE TO LIVE BECAUSE OF POVERTY OR DISASTER

MAJOR A LEVEL OF RANK IN THE ARMY

MATE A SLANG TERM FOR "FRIEND" COMMONLY USED IN GREAT BRITAIN AND AUSTRALIA

MICRO-GRANTS A SMALL AMOUNT OF MONEY GIVEN TO PEOPLE IN NEED TO HELP START A BUSINESS, GO BACK TO SCHOOL, OR BETTER THEIR LIVES IN SOME WAY

MISSION A PLACE THAT PROVIDES FOOD AND SHELTER TO PEOPLE IN NEED

NEGLECTED NOT GIVEN THE PROPER CARE AND TREATMENT FOR SURVIVAL

ORPHAN A PERSON WITHOUT PARENTS OR CAREGIVERS

PGA THE PROFESSIONAL GOLFERS' ASSOCIATION

POUNDS ONE OF THE KINDS OF MONEY USED IN GREAT BRITAIN

POVERTY BEING POOR; HAVING VERY LITTLE MONEY OR THINGS

RADIATION A CANCER TREATMENT WHERE A PATIENT IS GIVEN HIGH DOSES OF ULTRAVIOLET LIGHT

REFUGEE SOMEONE WHO HAS HAD TO TAKE SHELTER AWAY FROM HOME BECAUSE OF WAR OR DISASTER

REVEREND A RELIGIOUS LEADER OF A CHURCH

SCHOLARSHIP A DONATION OF MONEY GIVE TO PAY FOR COLLEGE OR UNIVERSITY

SHELTER A PLACE WHERE PEOPLE IN NEED CAN COME TO GET FOOD OR SHELTER

SOMALIA A COUNTRY IN EASTERN AFRICA, NEAR KENYA AND ETHIOPIA

SPCA THE "SOCIETY FOR THE PREVENTION OF CRUELTY TO ANIMALS"

TOURNAMENT A LARGE, ORGANIZED EVENT, USUALLY FOR SPORTS

INDEX